AROUND THE WORLD

WITH

Disney

clockwise from top left:
WALT DISNEY WORLD RESORT, DISNEYLAND,
TOKYO DISNEYLAND RESORT, DISNEYLAND RESORT PARIS

AROUND THE WORLD WITH Disney

BY KEVIN MARKEY

DISNEY EDITIONS

New York

A ROUNDTABLE PRESS BOOK
New York

EDITIONS

For information address Disney Editions, 114 Fifth Avenue, New York, New York 10011–5690.

Written by Kevin Markey

Special thanks to Gregory Gujda, Claire Robinson (Corporate Administration); Quynh Kimball (Disney Design Group); Margaret Adamic (Disney Publishing); Pat Harris, Frankie LoBono (Disneyland Resort); Anna D'Arras, Christine Tweedly (Disneyland Resort Paris); Greg Albrecht, Masayo Enomoto, John Kavelin, Ed Storin (Tokyo Disneyland Resort); Dave Smith, Robert Tieman (Walt Disney Archives); Denise R. Brown, Mike Jusko, Diane Scoglio, Neil Small, David Stern, Marilyn Waters, Dave Fisher, Susan Zavala (Walt Disney Imagineering); Janice Hilliard, Cathy Moorefield, Nathan Rasmussen, Betsy Singer, Melora Watson (Walt Disney Parks and Resorts); Alyce Diamandis, Trish Nicolo, Darlene Papalini, Laura Simpson, Jeff Titelius (Walt Disney World Synergy); and Jill Safro. No thanks to Charley, Frances, Ivan, and Jeanne. Welcome Maya George Glenn and Penelope Park.

Printed in China

Some of the photographs for this book were taken by:
Vincent Begon: pages 123 (Peter Pan's Flight), 141 ("it's a small world," bottom right), 156 (Space Mountain, top right). Alain Boniec: pages 120–21 (Dumbo the Flying Elephant). Scott Brinegar: pages 18, 19 (Sleeping Beauty Castle). Sylvain Cambon: pages 59 (Indiana Jones and the Temple of Peril: Backwards!), 89 (Phantom Manor), 99 (Molly Brown and the Rivers of the Far West), 159 (Orbitron). Gene Duncan: pages 12, 13 (Cinderella Castle). Chieko Ishizawa: page 141 ("it's a small world," bottom left). Gary Krueger: page 32 (Le Carrousel de Lancelot). Vincent LeLoup: page 117 (Moteurs). Jean Christophe Moreau: page 24 (Alice's Curious Labyrinth, inset bottom). Eric Morency: pages 25 (Le Pays des Contes de Fées), 66 (Disneyland Paris Railroad), 69 (Big Thunder Mountain Railroad, inset top right), 156 (Space Mountain, bottom). James D. Morgan: page 23 (Le Château de la Belle au Bois Dormant). Martine Mouchy: page 24 (Alice's Curious Labyrinth). Takeshi Obara: pages 21 (Cinderella Castle), 51 (Jungle Cruise). David Roark: pages 14 (Cinderella Castle), 70–71 (Spaceship Earth with monorail). Philippe Rolle: pages 22 (La Tanière du Dragon), 93 (Pirates of the Caribbean, top right). Jill Safro: pages 48–49 (Jungle Cruise), 112 (Mr. Toad's Wild Ride, top right), 114 (Tuck & Roll's Drive'Em Buggies), 125 (Flik's Flyers, top). TIBO: page 82 (Le Légende de Buffalo Bill–Wild West Show). David Valdez: page 130 (Tree of Life, right).

For Disney Editions	**For Roundtable Press, Inc.**
Editorial Director: Wendy Lefkon	Directors: Marsha Melnick, Julie Merberg
Editor: Jody Revenson	Editor: John Glenn
	Designer: Jon Glick

Library of Congress Cataloging-in-Publication Data on file.
ISBN: 0-7868-5446-4
First Edition

opposite: Cinderella Castle, WALT DISNEY WORLD RESORT

AROUND THE WORLD WITH Disney

INTRODUCTION

ONE MAN'S DREAM. It's the name of a Disney-MGM Studios attraction about the life of Walt Disney, but the title could just as easily apply to all of Walt Disney World and its sister resorts around the world. For it was Walt's singular dream to build a place that would be a world unto itself, a wondrous land where people from all walks of life could come together in the pursuit of happiness.

"Walt Disney World is a tribute to the philosophy and life of Walter Elias Disney," said Walt's brother Roy O. Disney when Magic Kingdom Park opened in Florida in 1971. "And to the talents, dedication, and the loyalty of the entire Disney organization that made Walt Disney's dream come true."

More than thirty years and many expansions later, the dream keeps growing and getting better. From Magic Kingdom Park, the wizardry has extended to *Epcot*®, Disney-MGM Studios, and Disney's Animal Kingdom. From Walt Disney World and Disneyland Resort in the United States, it has been carried around the world, to France's Disneyland Resort Paris and to Tokyo Disneyland Resort and Tokyo DisneySea in Japan. The dream lives in strolling characters, joy-filled shows, and jaw-dropping attractions, in nostalgic re-creations of the past, and visionary looks at the future. Most vividly of all, it's alive in the smiles and laughter of millions of guests touched by the magic of Walt's dream.

opposite: **Main Street, U.S.A.,** Walt Disney World Resort

background: **Cinderella Castle,** WALT DISNEY WORLD RESORT
inset top: **Sleeping Beauty Castle,** DISNEYLAND
inset bottom: **Grizzly Peak,** DISNEY'S CALIFORNIA ADVENTURE

opposite from top: **Le Château de la Belle au Bois Dormant,**
DISNEYLAND RESORT PARIS; **Cinderella Castle,** TOKYO DISNEYLAND;
Sleeping Beauty Castle, HONG KONG DISNEYLAND

Worldwide Outreach for The Walt Disney Company

CELEBRATING 50 YEARS OF WISHES

Walt Disney once described Disneyland's Fantasyland as "the world of imagination, hopes, and dreams." Since 1948, when Walt and his animators designed the Toys for Tots train logo still in use today, to the present day as Disney characters deliver gifts and cheer to children in hospitals around the world, we have believed in making the dreams of children and families come true.

Each year, Disney makes dreams come true through partnerships with wish-granting organizations such as the Make-A-Wish Foundation®. Make-A-Wish, the largest wish-granting partner of DisneyHand, grants the wishes of children with life-threatening illnesses to enrich the human experience with strength, hope, and joy. The number one wish of all children they serve is a trip to a Disney park. In 2005, Disney will Celebrate 50 Years of Wishes by making the 50,000th Disney theme park wish come true, exactly 25 years after we fulfilled the wish of the very first Make-A-Wish child…a trip to Disneyland.

HAPPIEST CELEBRATION ON EARTH

On July 17, 1955, Disneyland opened its doors—and the rest is history. Fifty years of magical, spectacular, fun-filled history. Since Disneyland's premiere, Walt Disney's dream of a new kind of family entertainment has expanded to eleven theme parks and two cruise ships. Now the Disney Resorts are joining together in an unprecedented, extraordinary global salute in honor of the park that started it all.

At Walt Disney World, we're celebrating this anniversary with a golden opportunity to relive cherished favorites, experience new thrills, and sneak a peek at attractions from other Disney parks. It's the Happiest Celebration on Earth, and you're invited! We went from castle to castle and brought over some of the most amazing Disney shows and attractions. And then we added a unique new attraction created just for Florida.

But it wasn't enough to just discuss our circumnavigation, we also had to show it, in what you now hold in your hands—the first-ever souvenir book that offers a glimpse of the many similar and divergent attractions in all the Disney theme parks. Enjoy a new class of "E" ticket ride (and no flash photography, please) as we take you *Around the World with Disney*.

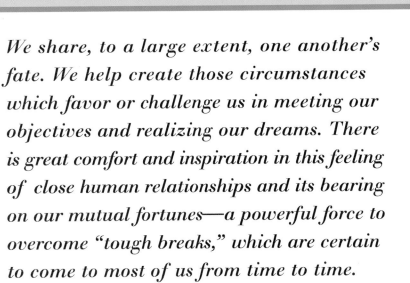

We share, to a large extent, one another's fate. We help create those circumstances which favor or challenge us in meeting our objectives and realizing our dreams. There is great comfort and inspiration in this feeling of close human relationships and its bearing on our mutual fortunes—a powerful force to overcome "tough breaks," which are certain to come to most of us from time to time.

—Walt Disney

For more information on DisneyHand's outreach projects and programs around the world, please visit us at www.DisneyHand.com.

CASTLES OF DREAMS

Every kingdom needs a castle. At Magic Kingdom Park the building takes the fanciful form of Cinderella Castle, whose golden spires rise toward the sky like wishes made on shooting stars. Each Magic Kingdom around the world has a castle of its own, and though architecture and names may differ from park to park—Sleeping Beauty Castle at Disneyland and Le Château de la Belle au Bois Dormant at Disneyland Resort Paris—they share a common purpose. Not to house any flesh-and-blood monarch, of course. That would be far too ordinary. What symbolically resides within their walls is more rare than royalty. It's nothing less than Disney magic. These wondrous dream palaces tell us that

Inspired by the palaces of medieval Europe, Cinderella Castle soars 189 feet above Magic Kingdom Park, a fantasy in three dimensions. A staircase inside leads to Cinderella's Royal Table, premier spot for character dining. Higher up, the castle contains a Disney family apartment, built according to Imagineer Herbert Ryman's original plans but never actually occupied. Models for the blue-turreted structure include Fontainebleu and Versailles in France and, most apt, the 1950 film *Cinderella.*

Mosaics at Cinderella Castle, Walt Disney World Resort

Facts hint at the wondrous visual effect of the Cinderella mosaics, but they don't really capture it: five stunning tile murals, 500 colors, real gold and silver highlights, and a million pieces of glass. Craftsmen even created special tints for the stepsisters' faces (red for rage and green for envy). Located in the castle breezeway, the handcrafted illustrations make a fitting introduction to Fantasyland, which lies just beyond.

Sleeping Beauty Castle, DISNEYLAND

The first Disney castle constructed is also the smallest, and there's a reason for that. The palaces that influenced its design—mad King Ludwig's Neuschwanstein in Bavaria, among others—were built large to awe and intimidate. Walt Disney wanted a more welcoming landmark. To create a sense of size without physical bulk, legendary designer Herb Ryman forced perspective by using large stones at the base and progressively smaller ones above. One thing Sleeping Beauty Castle does have in common with Neuschwanstein (the name means "new swan stone" in German) is the swans who often take up residence in the Disneyland moat.

Cinderella Castle, TOKYO DISNEYLAND

The exterior of Cinderella Castle at Tokyo Disneyland reproduces (albeit shorter) the Walt Disney World original right to the tips of its spires. Inside, a different story unfolds. Here guests find the Cinderella Mystery Castle Tour, an interactive show featuring a host of Disney villains.

Le Château de la Belle au Bois Dormant, DISNEYLAND RESORT PARIS

More fanciful than any of its sister structures, the delicately spired castle for Sleeping Beauty at Disneyland Resort Paris looks pretty in pink. Not to mention ivory, green, and gold. Another surprise awaits in the basement—La Tanière du Dragon (The Dragon's Lair), complete with a steam-spouting Audio-Animatronics dragon.

Alice's Curious Labyrinth, DISNEYLAND RESORT PARIS

Inspired by the stories of Lewis Carroll, this befuddling outdoor topiary maze at Disneyland Resort Paris contains a world of make-believe, including the castle of the Queen of Hearts.

Storybook Land Canal Boats, Disneyland, **and Le Pays des Contes de Fées,** Disneyland Resort Paris

At Disneyland, cruise boats transport guests into a miniature world, where Cinderella's castle sits atop a hill just around a river bend from Aladdin's intricately detailed Agrabah palace. At Disneyland Resort Paris, the attraction has a different name, Le Pays des Contes de Fées, but the dreamy effect is the same.

ROUND & ROUND WE GO

When Walt Disney's daughters were young, he often took them to Griffith Park in Los Angeles to ride the merry-go-round. Recalling those visits years later, he made sure his parks had their own vintage carousels. Featuring prancing horses, old-fashioned organ music, and hand-painted backgrounds, carousels embody the simple charms of the Victorian age. The link with history surely meant a lot to Walt, as did the fact that carousels appeal clear across generational lines. Grandparents love a spin on one as much as small children do. From Mad Tea Party to the Orange Stinger at Disney's California Adventure, the parks offer many variations on the carousel theme. Which just goes to show you that at Disney, what goes around definitely comes around.

overleaf & these pages: **Cinderella's Golden Carrousel,** Walt Disney World Resort
Built in 1917, this vintage carousel was rescued from a New Jersey amusement park. Imagineers completely restored the Victorian attraction, recasting some of the carved wooden figures and adding 18 hand-painted scenes from *Cinderella.* Like snowflakes, each of the 90 gently trotting horses is unique.

28

King Arthur Carrousel, DISNEYLAND

The Fantasyland centerpiece at Disneyland, a treasure from the golden age of carousels, was crafted by the legendary Dentzel Company in 1875. A total of 68 horses leap and prance in 17 rows, each animal different from the others, on one of the largest carousels in the world.

opposite: **Le Carrousel de Lancelot,** DISNEYLAND RESORT PARIS
Eighty-six steeds fit for a knight trot around the Knights of the Round Table–themed carousel at Disneyland Resort Paris.

below: **Caravan Carousel,** TOKYO DISNEYSEA
In the Arabian Coast section of Tokyo DisneySea, camels and Arabian stallions gallivant beneath the Moorish dome of the first double-decker Disney carousel.

King Triton's Carousel, DISNEY'S CALIFORNIA ADVENTURE

At the heart of Paradise Pier, 56 hand-carved sea horses, dolphins, otters, and other creatures native to the California coast wend their merry way around King Triton's Carousel. The Pacific marine theme is carried to the music as well: instead of traditional Tin Pan Alley tunes, the classic band organ tootles Beach Boys hits.

Mad Tea Party, WALT DISNEY WORLD RESORT

No wonder the Mad Hatter's so loopy: a ride in one of these giant twirling teacups is enough to make anyone dizzy. Inspired by the Unbirthday Party in the 1951 film *Alice in Wonderland*, this joyride lets guests control the speed of their spins, making it a perfect cup of tea for riders of all tastes.

above left & above: **Orange Stinger,** DISNEY'S CALIFORNIA ADVENTURE

A swing ride with a twist, Orange Stinger operates inside a giant orange peel at Disney's California Adventure. As 48 single-seat swings pick up speed, a drone of bumblebees in flight grows louder, and the scent of fresh oranges fills the air.

opposite: **Sun Wheel,** DISNEY'S CALIFORNIA ADVENTURE

Don't be fooled by the benignly smiling sun face. The 170-foot-tall Sun Wheel at Disney's California Adventure turns the traditional Ferris wheel experience on its head. Literally. Sixteen of the iconic attraction's 24 six-person gondolas slide in, out, and around tracks mounted within the massive outer ring. Upon completing a 500-foot circumnavigation, passengers can be forgiven for not knowing which end is up.

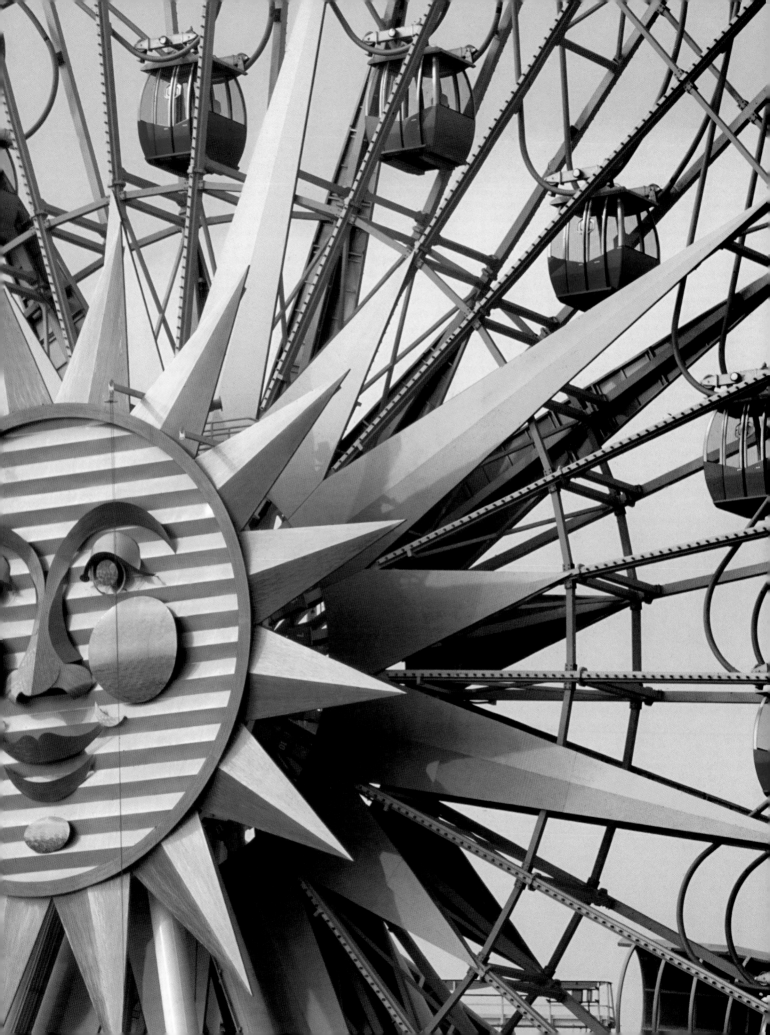

LEADING

LADIES

"Since the beginning of mankind," Walt Disney once said, explaining the importance of fairy tales, "the fable-tellers have not only given us entertainment but a kind of wisdom, humor, and understanding that, like all true art, remains imperishable through the ages." At the heart of all the best fairy tales, of course, stands a princess. Innocent, kind, noble in spirit as well as name, these timeless characters personify all that's best in each of us. They represent the hopes and wishes of childhood. To meet such friends in person is a dream come true for fans of every age.

above: **Cinderella Wishing Well and Cinderella Fountain,** WALT DISNEY WORLD RESORT

Tucked neatly beside the path from Fantasyland to Tomorrowland, the Cinderella Wishing Well offers great castle views. Befitting its mistress's big heart and humble origins, coins collected from within are donated to children's charities. An alcove in the Castle's rear courtyard contains another enchanting place to make a wish or pop the question—the Cinderella Fountain. The future princess sits atop a bubbling fountain, a crown just visible in the tracery behind her head. When guests bend to make an offer, the crown appears to settle on her head, hence the fountain's nickname—"Rags to Riches."

opposite: **Cinderellabration,** WALT DISNEY WORLD RESORT

Picking up where the classic animated film left off, this spectacular musical writes a new chapter in Cinderella's happily-ever-after story. Performing on the stage in front of Cinderella Castle in the Magic Kingdom, a cast of elaborately costumed characters bring to life the coronation that follows the Disney Princess's royal wedding to her Prince. The show was first staged at Tokyo Disneyland, where it became an instant guest favorite.

above: **Ariel's Grotto (and Triton Gardens),** Walt Disney World Resort, Disneyland
The Little Mermaid receives guests amid starfish and waterfalls in her
Fantasyland hideaway, posing for snapshots and signing autographs. Young
fans can also test the waters of a fountain-filled play area. In the Disneyland
version, King Triton's youngest daughter sings of her desire to become "Part
of Your World." Nearby, the dancing waters of Triton's Garden put on a show
of their own.

opposite & chapter opener bottom left: **Voyage of the Little Mermaid,** Walt Disney World Resort
Combining animation, live action, puppetry, and special effects, this Disney-
MGM Studios multimedia show unfolds in a theater designed to resemble
King Triton's underwater realm. As the evil Ursula plots to get her tentacles
around Ariel's voice, Prince Eric, Flounder, and Sebastian come to the aid of
the princess.

above & chapter opener top right: **Storytime with Belle at Fairytale Garden,**
WALT DISNEY WORLD RESORT

A hush falls over the small crowd when Belle arrives on this intimate outdoor
stage. Fresh from her timeless adventure, the heroine of *Beauty and the Beast*
recounts her tale, inviting lucky fans to help with the telling.

opposite: **Beauty and the Beast—Live on Stage,** WALT DISNEY WORLD RESORT

Before the Broadway smash, there was "Beauty and the Beast—Live on Stage."
Presented in the plush Theater of the Stars at Disney-MGM Studios, this live-
action musical re-enacts in song and dance one of the greatest love stories
ever told.

Snow White Grotto, DISNEYLAND

Marble statues of Snow White and her Dwarfs beckon from a serene grotto to the right of Sleeping Beauty Castle. Carved in Italy, the figures have greeted Disneyland guests since 1961. Above the gentle splashing of the waterfall, the voice of Snow White rises in song from the Grotto's Wishing Well. The recording of "I'm Wishing" was made by the actress who voiced Snow White in the 1937 film.

Snow White's Scary Adventures, WALT DISNEY WORLD RESORT
Released in 1937, *Snow White and the Seven Dwarfs* was the world's first
full-length animated movie, which makes the fair maiden Disney's original
princess. As in the beloved movie, Snow White's heart-pounding journey
through the Evil Queen's forest leads to a happy ending with her prince.

It's no surprise that Adventureland was one of the original Disneyland areas in 1955. Whisking off to exotic locales has always been essential to the Disney experience. The original big trip was Jungle Cruise. Today, that Audio-Animatronics attraction and its spiritual descendant, the live-animal Kilimanjaro Safaris at Disney's Animal Kingdom Park, continue to take guests deep into the animal world. Other adventures transcend the natural world, transporting armchair travelers everywhere from the middle of an Indiana Jones™ movie to Pooh's Hundred Acre Wood on a blustery day. "Always, when you travel, assimilate the sights and the sounds of the world," Walt Disney once advised. To which we might add, "and hold on to your hat. You're in for a wild ride."

JOURNEYS OF ADVENTURE

Jungle Cruise, WALT DISNEY WORLD RESORT
As impressive as the Audio-Animatronics menagerie
is the landscaping surrounding it. A triumph of the
Imagineer's art, Jungle Cruise re-creates sections
of the Nile river valley, Amazonian rain forests,
Cambodian jungles, and African veldts—and packs
them all into a few outrageously lush acres. Unlike
nature, it also lets you see the back side of the water.

above & chapter opener: **Jungle Cruise,** Disneyland

If Imagineers ever questioned the feasibility of turning a piece of arid southern California into tropical jungle, they didn't let on to Walt. He repeatedly plugged Jungle Cruise on TV while Disneyland was little more than a blueprint. When the park opened in 1955, guests mobbed the attraction they'd heard so much about. Jungle Cruise has been a favorite ever since—for the bathing elephants and hungry lions, to be sure, but just as much for the timelessly corny spiels of the tour boat guides.

left: **Jungle Cruise,** Tokyo Disneyland

Tokyo Disneyland has its own version of Jungle Cruise, but Disneyland Resort Paris does not. The 1955 Anaheim original spawned so many European imitations in the 1960s and 1970s that the attraction was left off the Paris blueprint.

51

DinoLand U.S.A., WALT DISNEY WORLD RESORT

Part paleontological dig, part roadside attraction, this prehistoric corner of Disney's Animal Kingdom is one place that encourages bonehead play. Junior archaeologists get to traipse through a fossil maze, clamber over dinosaur climbing structures, and dig for skeletal remains in a huge sandpit. The sculpted skeleton of a giant 50-foot tall brachiosaurus straddles the entrance above "Oldengate Bridge."

Dinosaur, WALT DISNEY WORLD RESORT

If voracious giant lizards don't get you in DinoLand U.S.A.'s time-traveling race against extinction, a pulverizing meteor shower may. Guests journey back 65 million years to rescue the last iguanodon, a relatively harmless 16-foot plant eater. Standing in the way is a fierce carnotaurus, among other toothy dinos, ready to turn time travelers into Cretaceous canapés. Meanwhile, a giant asteroid hurtles toward earth. When it strikes, it'll be curtains for the dinosaurs—and any visitors who don't get back to the future.

above: **Primeval Whirl,** WALT DISNEY WORLD RESORT

A tight-twisting kiddie coaster with more dips than a roadside ice cream stand, Primeval Whirl turns paleontology into child's play.

right: **Chester & Hester's Dino-Rama!,** WALT DISNEY WORLD RESORT

Fun will never become extinct at Chester and Hester's Dino-Rama!, a mom-and-pop carnival straight off Route 66. With its dinosaur-themed games and retro rides, the park within a park packs the wallop of a T-Rex.

The Many Adventures of Winnie the Pooh, WALT DISNEY WORLD RESORT

With the tubby little cubby leading the way, guests pile into honey pots for a whirl through the Hundred Acre Wood. The day turns blustery, water rises alarmingly in the floody place, a heffalump makes a rare appearance: scenes lovingly drawn from Disney's beloved movies and the books that inspired them. As in the stories, things end sweetly for honey-hungry Pooh, bear of little brain, big stomach, and bigger heart.

Kilimanjaro Safaris Expedition, Walt Disney World Resort

The World's wildest attraction—literally. Open-sided jitneys truck animal lovers through a 100-acre park painstakingly landscaped to recall the African savanna. Zebras graze in lush grasslands, hippos wallow in ponds, and lions laze in the sun. Invisible barriers separate predators from prey, but the illusion of openness is complete. A peaceful outing in the green safari vehicles that run on propane turns dangerous when guides spot traces of elephant poachers and give chase over rutted tracks.

page: **Indiana Jones™ Epic Stunt Spectacular!,** WALT DISNEY WORLD RESORT
Earthquakes, runaway boulders, massive fireballs? All in a day's work for
Indiana Jones™—and audiences of Disney-MGM Studio's jaw-dropping
thirty-minute FX show. Hollywood stunt pros re-create scenes from the first
film, revealing the art behind the movie illusions.

inset: **Indiana Jones™ Adventure,** DISNEYLAND
Those who penetrate the inner sanctum of this jungle temple will be granted
one of three wishes: enormous wealth, eternal youth, or knowledge of the
future. Nice idea, but the truth of the matter is that no one has ever made it
out of the temple alive. Undeterred, guests set off in jeeps, following Indy
through a maze of lava pits, collapsing caverns, and snake-filled recesses.
(Did we mention Indy hates snakes?)

below: **Indiana Jones™ Adventure: Temple of the Crystal Skull,** Tokyo DisneySea

In Tokyo, the object of Indy's quest is the Fountain of Youth. Finding it on a map and actually reaching it are two different things, of course. The fabled spa is buried deep within an ancient pyramid, guarded by the fire-breathing Crystal Skull.

inset: **Indiana Jones™ and the Temple of Peril: Backwards!,** Disneyland Resort Paris

Before the first ascent of this Disneyland Resort Paris roller coaster, passengers cross an abandoned dig site. One wonders what happened to the archaeological party. Before any answers are offered, guests find themselves shooting up the tracks—backward.

Matterhorn Bobsleds, DISNEYLAND

At 147 feet tall, the Matterhorn in Disneyland is the tallest mountain in the park—about 1/100th the size of its Swiss namesake. Inspired by the live-action film *Third Man on the Mountain*, the roller coaster opened as Disneyland's first thrill ride in 1959. Two decades later, Imagineers installed a blazing-eyed Abominable Snowman at the summit.

Journey to the Center of the Earth, Tokyo DisneySea
Perched atop Mysterious Island at Tokyo DisneySea, this Jules Verne–themed roller coaster plunges through a volcanic crater into a subterranean twilight zone.

Expedition EVEREST, Walt Disney World Resort
Walt Disney World finally gets an Abominable Snowman of its own in 2006, when Expedition EVEREST opens in the Asia section of Disney's Animal Kingdom. The coasterlike, high-speed train adventure shoots guests up a 200-foot-high mountain. On the way to the peak, they climb through a bamboo forest, skirt plunging cliffs, and race through ice caverns—all prefatory to an encounter with the legendary Yeti.

RIDING
THE RAILS

Trains so fascinated Walt that he built a scale model railway in the backyard of his Los Angeles home, dubbing it the Carolwood Pacific after the name of his street. Insistent that train rides be a central part of Disneyland and, later, Walt Disney World, he sent his Imagineers to scour the four corners of the earth for vintage steam engines. They returned with banana trains from Latin America, sugar cane–hauling cars from Louisiana, and a locomotive retired from heavy duty at a New England lumber mill. Other Disney iron horses are pure park originals, of course, such as Big Thunder Mountain Railroad. You won't find the likes of it anywhere outside Frontierland.

Disneyland Railroad, DISNEYLAND

Between Tomorrowland and Main Street stations, the quartet of steam locomotives at Disneyland chug through several hidden gems, including a Grand Canyon diorama and Primeval World, featuring the first Audio-Animatronics dinosaurs created. Two of the engines, the *E. P. Ripley* and the *C. K. Holliday*, were built for the park at the Disney Studio. The other two, the *Fred C. Gurley* and the *Ernest S. March*, are salvaged historic models. All four are named for American railroad executives.

No mere playthings, the four antique steam engines of the Walt Disney World Railroad enjoyed long working lives hauling passengers and freight in Mexico. Disney Imagineers bought the locomotives in 1969, completely refurbishing them for the Magic Kingdom. The names of three of the four will be familiar to any Disneyphile—Walter E. Disney, Roy O. Disney, and Lilly Belle (for Walt's wife, Lillian). But who, you may ask, is Roger Broggie? Railroad buff and Imagineer, he's the man who helped Walt install the scale model railroad in his backyard.

Disneyland Railroad, DISNEYLAND RESORT PARIS

Each of the four Disneyland Resort Paris trains consists of a brass-fitted steam locomotive, a tender, and five passenger cars. Built in Britain to authentic nineteenth-century standards, all except one of the iron horses are named for historic American figures: W. F. (Buffalo Bill) Cody, C. K. Holliday (after the founder of the Santa Fe Railroad, instrumental in opening the West), and the G. Washington. The fourth is called Eureka, the Greek word for "I found it!" The name refers to the discovery of gold at Sutter's Mill in 1848—and the subsequent train-borne rush of prospectors into California.

Wildlife Express, WALT DISNEY WORLD RESORT
Styled after a British steam locomotive built for service in Africa more than a century ago, Wildlife Express chuffs between the village of Harambe and Rafiki's Planet Watch in Africa. On the way, passengers are treated to a backstage peek at Disney's Animal Kingdom Park.

above & opposite: **Big Thunder Mountain Railroad,** Walt Disney World Resort

An Imagineering tour de force, the Frontierland roller coaster lovingly re-creates a Wild West landscape on 2.5 acres. It took two years and 650 tons of steel for workers to add the details of a gold-mining village, bat-filled cavern, hot springs, and sandstone buttes. Memories of the lavishly themed attraction? They last forever.

inset clockwise: **Big Thunder Mountain Railroad,** Tokyo Disneyland, Disneyland, Disneyland Resort Paris

Big Thunder Mountain at Disneyland is not only the first (1979), it's also the only one modeled after Utah's Bryce Canyon National Park. Versions built for Walt Disney World (1980), Tokyo Disneyland (1987), and Disneyland Resort Paris (1992) take inspiration from the red sandstone formations of Monument Valley on the Arizona-Utah border.

right: **DisneySea Electric Railway,** Tokyo DisneySea

A replica of a nineteenth-century American streetcar, this two-car elevated trolley shuttles between the American Waterfront and Port Discovery sections of Tokyo DisneySea.

Monorail, WALT DISNEY WORLD RESORT

Part attraction, part transportation system, all Disney. Since opening day in 1971, the Walt Disney World Monorail has shuttled more than a billion passengers along 14 miles of track. In Anaheim, the Disneyland Monorail debuted at Tomorrowland in 1959. Within two years, America's first daily operating monorail became a bona fide mass transit carrier—and the first monorail to cross a public street anywhere in the country when the line was extended to the Disneyland Hotel.

Jolly Trolley, DISNEYLAND
A smooth operator it's not—the Jolly Trolley lurches, jerks, and wobbles from one end of Toon Town to the other. The secret of its *loco* motion? Uneven wheels.

above: **Casey Jr. Circus Train,** Disneyland

Inspired by the circus train from *Dumbo*, the little engine that could whistles around Storybook Land. A Disneyland exclusive since 1955.

left: **Heimlich's Chew Chew Train,** Disney's California Adventure

The insatiable caterpillar from *A Bug's Life* takes guests for a fragrant ride as he forages in a bug's land. When Heimlich gobbles through a giant watermelon (as in the movie, all is seen from a bug's perspective), passengers are spritzed with aromatic juice. When he nibbles a box of animal crackers, a vanilla scent fills the air.

THE SPIRIT OF AMERICA

In this most American of places, every day is a little bit like the Fourth of July. Marching bands parade down Main Street, Old Glory flutters in the breeze, and after dark, fireworks explode in a colorful spectacle. As famous as he was for dreaming up unforgettable characters and magical attractions, Walt Disney was equally renowned for his proud patriotism. "If you could see close in my eyes," he once avowed, "the American flag is waving in both of them and up my spine is growing this red, white, and blue stripe." Those American true colors suffuse Walt Disney World.

overleaf & left: **Main Street, U.S.A.,** WALT DISNEY WORLD RESORT

It's been called a step back in time, a trip down memory lane to a place where life moves at the leisurely clip of a horse-drawn trolley. Inspired in part by Marceline, Missouri, the hamlet where Walt grew up, Main Street, U.S.A., evokes an old-time America of general stores, ice cream parlors, and corner barbershops where candy-striped quartets never hit a sour note.

below & inset: **Town Square Exposition Hall,** WALT DISNEY WORLD RESORT

Main Street, U.S.A.'s stateliest building, ornate Town Square Exhibition Hall houses a shrine to photography. The museum-quality installation documents the evolution of the art, while "Steamboat Willie" and other seminal Disney cartoons flicker on screen. Speaking of pictures, the Goofy sculpture by the front door makes a great photo op.

Liberty Square, Walt Disney World Resort

Every day is Independence Day at Liberty Square, Colonial setting of The Hall of Presidents, the *Liberty Belle* steamship, and the magnificent Liberty Tree, living symbol of freedom. Festooned with thirteen Paul Revere–style lanterns, representing the original colonies, the 135-year-old live oak was discovered on the Disney property and transplanted to the square. At 40 feet high, 30 feet wide, and weighing nearly 40 tons, it's the largest living thing at Walt Disney World.

The Hall of Presidents, WALT DISNEY WORLD RESORT

All the chief executives appear in Audio-Animatronics form in this classic
attraction, possibly the greatest political gathering since the forefathers
framed the Constitution. To nail every detail, Disney designers scoured
history books for information on period textiles, tailoring, jewelry, shoes,
and hairstyles. Every figure has a change of clothes.

The Walt Disney Story, Featuring "Great Moments with Mr. Lincoln,"
DISNEYLAND

Walt Disney's personal fascination with the sixteenth president dates to his childhood, when he made a Lincoln costume and wore it to school. As an adult, he created "Great Moments," a stirring homage to the Great Emancipator, for the 1964–1965 New York World's Fair, which then moved to the Opera House at Disneyland. Lincoln's face is re-created from a life mask of the actual man made in 1860.

American Waterfront, Tokyo DisneySea
A celebration of bustling East Coast harbors circa 1912, this section of Tokyo DisneySea includes Hudson Docks, inside the Port of New York, and Cape Cod, home to the DisneySea Transit Steamer Line, among other salty attractions.

Tom Sawyer Island, Walt Disney World Resort

From the pages of the Great American novel springs a playground of caves, creaky bridges, and wooded trails. In best Tom and Huck fashion, guests reach the shores of this Rivers of America retreat on planked rafts. Amid the wilderness, Aunt Polly's Dockside Inn serves a decidedly civilized lemonade.

Le Légende de Buffalo Bill—Wild West Show, DISNEYLAND RESORT PARIS
Cowboy fever is alive and well in Paris. More than 100 years after Buffalo Bill Cody took Europe by storm, this rip-roaring dinner show packs its own permanent arena twice nightly in Disney Village at Disneyland Resort Paris. As in the original, genuine cowboys and Native Americans perform dazzling feats of riding, roping, and shooting.

Grizzly Peak, Disney's California Adventure

You've heard of the bear going over the mountain? Here, the bear *is* the mountain. Grizzly Peak, symbol of Disney's California Adventure Park, represents the untamable beauty of California's great national parks, such as Yosemite and Sequoia. Pine trees and sequoias grow on the lower slopes of the 110-foot peak.

The American Adventure, WALT DISNEY WORLD RESORT

It took 110,000 bricks to build the Georgian mansion that contains this
Epcot® World Showcase tour de force, each one of them cast by hand.
A lot of work? Sure. But nothing compared to building a nation, the subject
of the awe-inspiring Audio-Animatronics spectacle. Speaking in voices
carefully re-created from the public record, more than twenty towering
figures, from Ben Franklin to Susan B. Anthony, and Frederick Douglass
to Rosie the Riveter, recall key events in American history.

With all the ghosts afoot, Walt Disney World truly is a happy haunting ground—emphasis on happy. Local ghouls tend to be a pretty upbeat bunch, less frightening than fun loving. Witness the song-and-dance antics of The Haunted Mansion's resident spooks. Even at their most mischievous, these irrepressible specters inspire awe rather than dread. Likewise not so frightening are the scruffy (and occasionally skeletal) buccaneers that haunt Pirates of the Caribbean. They may be greedy and gluttonous, but they're really just there to steal a laugh. They're also improper, unruly, and gleefully mud-covered—clearly enjoying their unpleasant career choice. Our high-spirited guys and ghouls will tempt you to drop in over and over again for a joyful time—as long as you don't mind the unpredictable drops at *The Twilight Zone Tower of Terror*™.

above & overleaf top left: **The Haunted Mansion,** Walt Disney World Resort

"When hinges creak in doorless chambers and strange and frightening sounds echo through the halls, whenever candle lights flicker, where the air is deathly still, that is the time when ghosts are present, practicing their terror with ghoulish delight." So begins a journey of 999 ghosts through arguably the most famous haunted house in the world. Certainly it's the most popular.

left: **The Haunted Mansion,** Disneyland

Before The Haunted Mansion opened at Disneyland in 1969, Walt Disney invited all homeless ghosts to come live there. In deciding what the house should look like, he overruled designers who wanted to give the exterior a run-down appearance. He said he would keep up the outside and let the ghosts take care of the interior. The narrator is Paul Frees, who voiced Ludwig Von Drake in Donald Duck cartoons.

Phantom Manor, Disneyland Resort Paris

Unlike its brick-and-stone American counterparts, the ornate, wood-frame buildings of Virginia City, Nevada, inspired the Disneyland Resort Paris version of The Haunted Mansion. The Old West theme makes sense, as Phantom Manor is located in Frontierland. The mansion, in its many forms, is the only attraction that is located in a different land in each Magic Kingdom Park. The Haunted Mansion at Tokyo Disneyland Resort was placed in Fantasyland.

chapter opener top right, this page left & opposite: **The Twilight Zone Tower of Terror™,**
WALT DISNEY WORLD RESORT

This creepy Disney-MGM Studios hotel looms larger than anything in Walt
Disney World (for the record, Big Thunder Mountain ranks second, while
Cinderella Castle places third). It's tops in popularity, too: guests recently voted
it the number one attraction. Programmable drop sequences ratchet up the
scare factor, creating random elevator plunges and making every ride unique.

above: **The Twilight Zone Tower of Terror™,** DISNEY'S CALIFORNIA ADVENTURE

At 183 feet, not only is the West Coast version of The Hollywood Tower Hotel
the highest building at the Disneyland Resort—it's the tallest in all of Anaheim.
Situated in the Hollywood Pictures Backlot area of Disney's California
Adventure, the star-crossed edifice features three elevator shafts (compared
with two at the Walt Disney World original) and is done up in a regionally
appropriate architectural style dubbed Pueblo Deco by Imagineers: a unique
blend of Southwest, Mission, and Art Deco elements.

Pirates of the Caribbean,
WALT DISNEY WORLD RESORT

Dead men may tell no tales, as the narrator to one of the World's all-time most popular attractions warns, but boy, do they act them out. As boats plunge guests into a maritime netherworld, irrepressible ruffians sing a chantey that sets a playful tone for all the hijinks that follow. Will that dog *ever* let go of the keys?

clockwise from top: **Pirates of the Caribbean,** DISNEYLAND, DISNEYLAND RESORT PARIS, TOKYO DISNEYLAND

When the original Pirates attraction opened in New Orleans Square at Disneyland in 1967, it was the most elaborate Audio-Animatronics attraction ever built. Since then, the ride has been duplicated in each of Disney's four Magic Kingdoms worldwide. Minor details differ from park to park, but the essentials remain the same: skeletons, cannon fire, widespread looting, and general mayhem playfully enacted by as colorful a cast of ruffians as ever sailed the seas. At Disneyland Resort Paris, the Pirates of the Caribbean restaurant is called Blue Lagoon. At Disneyland and Tokyo Disneyland, it's known as Blue Bayou.

WATER WHERE

Every child learns that water covers 70 percent of the world's surface, but what of Walt Disney World? Well, not quite that much, but a significant portion. Bay Lake alone encompasses 450 acres. Add Seven Seas Lagoon, Rivers of America, Boardwalk's Crescent Lake, World Showcase Lagoon, and the other waterways that wind through the parks, and you've got a kingdom fit for Ariel, the Little Mermaid. Not to mention myriad other aquatic attractions. Truth be told, Disney designers demonstrated a maritime flair even before coming to wet central Florida. In 1955, Canal Boats of the World and *Mark Twain* Riverboat counted among Disneyland's original attractions.

overleaf & opposite: **Splash Mountain,** WALT DISNEY WORLD RESORT

Combining Brer Rabbit and friends from the 1946 animated film *Song of the South* with a white-knuckle flume ride, this Frontierland favorite puts the zip in "Zip-a-Dee-Doo-Dah." The wet and woolly log ride features wonderful music and more than 100 Audio-Animatronics figures, though guests can be forgiven if they're distracted by what awaits near the end: a five-story plunge at a 45-degree angle into a briar-girded pond. According to company legend, Disney Imagineer Tony Baxter came up with the idea for fast, fun Splash Mountain while fuming in traffic on the way to work.

above. left to right: **Splash Mountain,** DISNEYLAND, TOKYO DISNEYLAND

At 52 feet, the final flume drop at Splash Mountain in Critter Country at Disneyland is two feet longer than the one at Walt Disney World. When it opened in 1989, it was the longest anywhere. The attraction is also an icon at Tokyo Disneyland. It began operating there in 1992, the same year it debuted at Walt Disney World.

Liberty Belle **Riverboat and the Rivers of America,** WALT DISNEY WORLD RESORT
From stem to stern, the *Liberty Belle* is a working riverboat. Just like the
paddleboats Mark Twain piloted down the Mississippi more than a century
ago, steam turns the paddle wheel, pushing the vessel through the water.
About the only thing Twain wouldn't recognize is the track at the bottom of
the Rivers of America that keeps the *Liberty Belle* on course as she steams
from Liberty Square past wildlife scenes along the shore of Frontierland.

top left: *Mark Twain* Riverboat and the Rivers of America, Disneyland
Constructed for Disneyland's 1955 opening, the *Mark Twain* Riverboat was the first paddle wheeler built in the United States in half a century. The 150-ton triple-decker plies the Rivers of America.

top right: *Mark Twain* Riverboat, Tokyo Disneyland
The paddle wheeler *Mark Twain* carries a bit of that old Mississippi magic to Tokyo Disneyland as it cruises around Rivers of America.

above left: *Molly Brown* Riverboat and the Rivers of the Far West,
Disneyland Resort Paris
At Disneyland Resort Paris, the *Molly Brown* joins the *Mark Twain*. Collectively known as the Thunder Mesa Riverboats, the vessels sail past Big Thunder Mountain, pioneer homesteads, and geysers on the Rivers of the Far West.

above right: Sailing Ship *Columbia*, Disneyland
Named for the eighteenth-century ship commanded by Robert Gray, the first American to circumnavigate the globe, the *Columbia* docks in Fowler's Harbor at New Orleans Square in Disneyland. When not cruising near Tom Sawyer Island, the floating museum of the great age of sail hoists the Jolly Roger as a pirate ship in "Fantasmic!"

left: Donald's Boat, Walt Disney World Resort
Good thing ducks are such strong swimmers: Donald's Boat, officially the *Miss Daisy*, leaks like a sieve. Young skippers love to splash in fountains surrounding the Mickey's Toontown Fair playscape. Inside, a whistle shoots water in the air.

Kali River Rapids, WALT DISNEY WORLD RESORT

What's in a name? Considering that Kali is the Hindu goddess of destruction, this white-water raft ride through Asia in Disney's Animal Kingdom lets riders off fairly easily. To be sure, passengers get tossed, turned, and soaked like socks in the wash cycle as rafts bounce through the rain forest and past temple ruins. But everybody arrives in one piece in the end. The same can't be said of the forest itself. During one terrifying stretch, outlaw loggers set an inferno raging through the wilderness.

Grizzly River Run, DISNEY'S CALIFORNIA ADVENTURE

The beauty of round rafts is that, as they plunge down a mountain torrent, they also spin. This ensures that Grizzly River Run (Grr for short), a centerpiece of Disney's California Adventure, always lives up to its motto: "The Wetter, the Better." Two steep drops into mountain gorges, including a stomach-lurching 21-footer, thundering waterfalls, and a series of billowing geysers don't hurt the cause.

above: **Venetian Gondolas,** Tokyo DisneySea

Just like its romantic Italian namesake, the Tokyo DisneySea version of Venice has canals instead of roads. Guests can sit back and enjoy enchanting views as gondoliers pole the ornate boats down narrow waterways, singing traditional Italian ballads as they go.

left: **DisneySea Transit Steamer Line,** Tokyo DisneySea

The covered, side-wheeler ferries of the Tokyo DisneySea Transit Steamer Line ferry passengers on scenic excursions around the park. Inspired by early nineteenth-century American steamboats, each of the fleet's 12 vessels is named for a famous adventurer.

above: **Aquatopia,** TOKYO DISNEYSEA

In this wild water ride at Tokyo DisneySea's fantasy futuristic Port Discovery, hovercraft-shaped vessels spin guests through a maze of whirlpools, waterspouts, geysers, and waterfalls. Think Disneyland's Autopia crossed with Jules Verne.

left & below: **Mermaid Lagoon,** TOKYO DISNEYSEA

King Triton happily rules one of seven watery ports within Tokyo DisneySea Mermaid Lagoon. The cartoonlike realm's seven under-the-sea attractions include Jumpin' Jellyfish swing ride, Ariel's Playground, Flounder's Flying Fish Coaster, and the Whirlpool, a Mad Tea Cup–style spin ride.

Typhoon Lagoon, WALT DISNEY WORLD RESORT

According to legend, the trawler marooned atop Mount Mayday, the *Miss Tilly*, arrived there courtesy of a perfect storm. It was swept out of the ironically named port of Safen Sound, Florida. Sounds fishy to us. But then, so does surfing in central Florida, and we know that happens on the ever-breaking waves of Typhoon Lagoon's massive surf pool. Other watery wonders include raft rides and waterslides, notably the 214-foot-long Humunga Kowabunga. On the latter, guests whip down a 52-foot drop like human torpedoes.

Blizzard Beach, WALT DISNEY WORLD RESORT

Disney's most intense water park takes the basic concept of the Winter Olympics and adds water. Toboggan runs become dipsy-doodling waterslides. Slalom courses turn into zigzagging chutes. Most jaw-dropping of all, the ski jump atop 120-foot-tall Mt. Gushmore morphs into Summit Plummet, the world's fastest free-fall speed slide—with nothing but a bathing suit between you and the elements. According to local legend, Disney built the ski resort after a freak blizzard hit Florida. Then, wouldn't you know it?, the weather warmed up again.

BUILT FOR

Before there was *FASTPASS*, there were fast attractions. Cars, coasters, and coasters designed to look like cars. They burn rubber around Walt Disney World race courses, hurtle down twisting steel tracks, and sprint through traditional indoor dark rides past scenery that is as surprising as every sudden turn in the road. Some of the best-loved automobile-themed attractions have roots (or should we say, routes?) that stretch back to Disneyland and the car culture of 1950s Southern California. Others were born of cutting-edge technology suitable for NASA or the laboratories of Detroit. Whatever their origins, Disney's blazing chariots satisfy a universal need for speed.

overleaf & above: **Tomorrowland Indy Speedway,** WALT DISNEY WORLD RESORT

These sleek racers have been zipping around a 2,200-foot-long Tomorrowland track since Magic Kingdom Park opened in 1971. Well, perhaps zipping is not the right word—the cars won't set any records. Kids love them at any speed, however. Must be the grown-up features, such as gas engines and rack-and-pinion steering.

opposite: **Autopia,** DISNEYLAND

With its realistic freeway signs, snazzy hot rods, and meandering raceway, Autopia at Disneyland has provided California kids with a license to drive since 1955.

inset opposite: **Grand Circuit Raceway,** TOKYO DISNEYLAND

As at the other parks, drivers at Tokyo Disneyland control speed as they wheel around the track in gas-powered cars. The only thing that's different is the name. Here Autopia goes by the name Grand Circuit Raceway.

California Screamin', DISNEY'S CALIFORNIA ADVENTURE

Forget a big hill. California Screamin', at Disney's California Adventure, uses a linear induction system to launch trains, taking them from 0 to 55 mph in less than five seconds. Other pertinent facts: the highest peak is 125 feet, the steepest drop is 50 degrees, the total track length is more than a mile, and a full invert is achieved on a loop that mirrors the face of a not-so-hidden Mickey.

Rock 'N Roller Coaster, WALT DISNEY WORLD RESORT

Rock 'N Roller Coaster rockets from a standstill to 60 mph in 2.8 seconds. Then comes the first loop and inversion, when guests strapped into stretch-limo–styled cars pull over four Gs. A state-of-the-art sound system wails all the while, every adrenaline-laced guitar lick blasting through 125 speakers. Rock on.

Mr. Toad's Wild Ride, DISNEYLAND

In speed-loving Mr. Toad's vintage roadster, guests race through cavernous Toad Hall, then crash through a wall and zoom into the streets and alleys of 1908 London. A Disneyland original, Toad is based on the 1949 animated film *The Adventures of Ichabod and Mr. Toad,* itself inspired by the classic children's book *The Wind in the Willows.*

Roger Rabbit's Car Toon Spin, Disneyland

Runaway taxicabs whisk passengers through Toontown in this high-speed homage to the Academy Award–winning 1988 film *Who Framed Roger Rabbit?* When it opened in 1994, Roger Rabbit's Car Toon Spin was Disneyland's first new dark ride in a decade. It remains the only one where guests can turn their own steering wheel to direct the ride vehicles.

Tuck and Roll's Drive 'Em Buggies, DISNEY'S CALIFORNIA ADVENTURE

Under P. T. Flea's big top in the a bug's land section of Disney's California Adventure, guests zip around in pill bug–shaped bumper cars. Collision-loving, gibberish-talking Tuck and Roll, stars of *A Bug's Life*, provide running commentary.

Mulholland Madness, Disney's California Adventure

Designed to recall the world-famous twists and dips of L.A.'s Mulholland Drive as it winds from the Hollywood Hills to Malibu, this steel coaster sends passengers careening around billboard-lined cliffs. Just when it looks as if passengers are about to go over an edge, the cars spin through a tight curve and race toward the next precipice.

opposite: **Test Track,** WALT DISNEY WORLD RESORT

On Detroit's legendary automobile proving grounds, engineers push machines to the limit. Through the wonder of Disney, guests get to go along for the ride. The longest, fastest thrill attraction at Walt Disney World subjects riders to extreme weather tests, rubber-burning brake tests, and spine-tingling feats of acceleration. At one point, the six-passenger vehicles rocket toward a crash barrier at 65 mph. When the ride ends, you'll have new respect for your car— assuming you ever want to get behind the wheel again.

above: **Moteurs...Action! Stunt Show Spectacular,** DISNEYLAND RESORT PARIS

At Walt Disney Studios Park in Paris, the French counterpart of Disney-MGM Studios, this high-octane, live-action special effects show keeps guests at the edges of their seats. And a lot of seats there are: the stadium has space for 3,000 fans, all eager to see how Hollywood designs, performs, and films thrilling stunts. An American version is scheduled to premiere at Disney-MGM Studios in 2005.

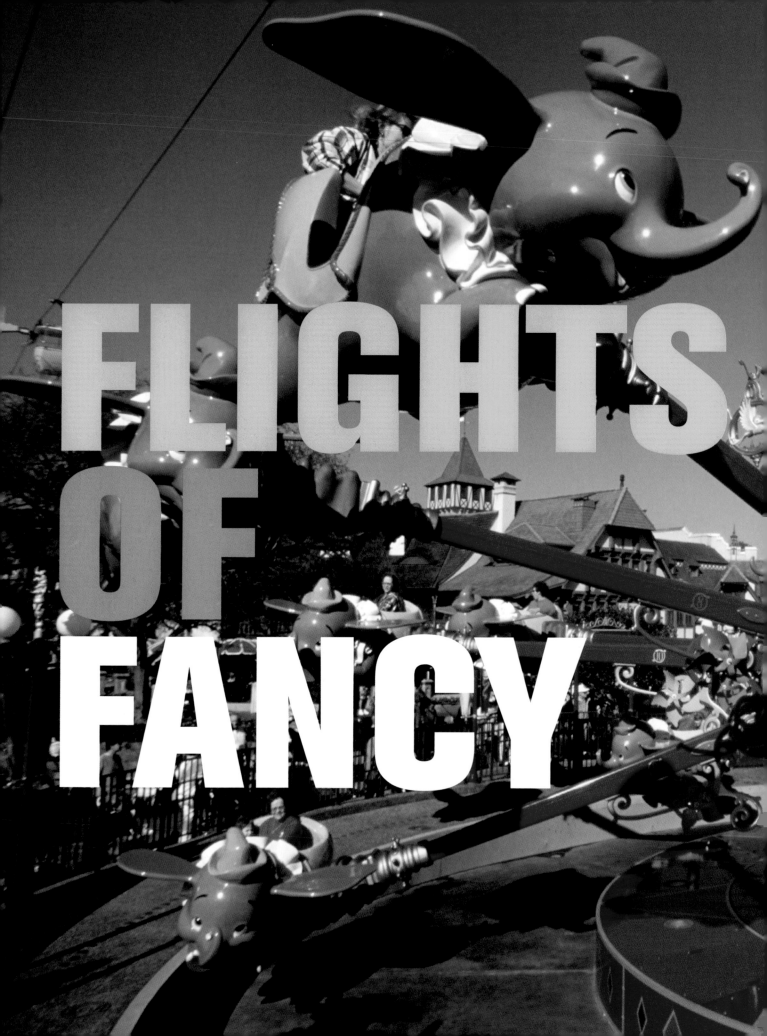

It should come as no surprise that Walt Disney World maintains the most diversified air fleet on earth—or more aptly, above it. After all, dreams do take flight here. The Parks' one-of-a-kind flying machines include everything from pachyderms that flutter like butterflies (Dumbo the Flying Elephant, a Disneyland original exported to Walt Disney World in 1971) to floor treatments that really put the throw in throw rug (The Magic Carpets of Aladdin). Guests can barnstorm with Goofy, shoot the moon with Peter Pan in a celestial pirate ship, and hang glide over the Golden Gate bridge. With all those nontraditional conveyances filling the happy skies, it's no wonder spirits run so high at Walt Disney World (and throughout the Disney universe), where Imagineers have always considered gravity a law that was made to be broken.

overleaf & right: **Dumbo the Flying Elephant,**
WALT DISNEY WORLD RESORT

A Fantasyland icon since Day One, Dumbo
glides above the park on broad, winglike
ears. Standing atop the hot-air balloon
at the center of the soaring elephant is
Timothy Q. Mouse, Dumbo's loyal friend
from the 1941 animated classic.

below: **The Magic Carpets of Aladdin,**
WALT DISNEY WORLD RESORT

In the heart of Adventureland's Agrabah
Bazaar, enchanted carpets take guests
for a spin around Genie's golden lamp.
Passengers control up-and-down and tilt
movements as they dodge streams of water
sprayed by spitting camels.

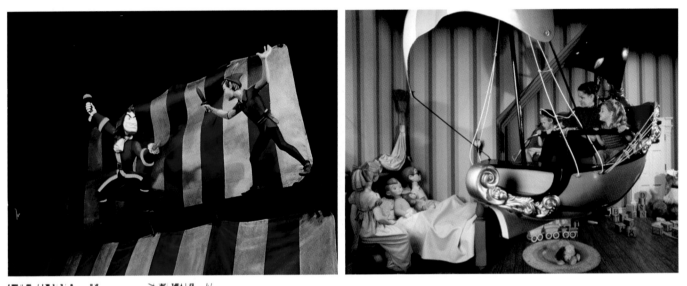

above left: **Peter Pan's Flight,** WALT DISNEY WORLD RESORT

Keep a good lookout for landmarks such as Big Ben and London Bridge as Peter Pan leads a night sortie over London in a pirate ship. Tinker Bell, Captain Hook, Wendy, Michael, and John all appear in this dreamy ride, which uses vehicles suspended from an overhead rail to simulate flight.

above right: **Peter Pan's Flight,** DISNEYLAND
opposite: **Peter Pan's Flight,** DISNEYLAND RESORT PARIS

At Disneyland, guests who listen carefully as they prepare to board the ship may hear Peter and Wendy laughing. From the bottom up, the blocks in the children's room spell Disney. In Paris, Peter Pan's Flight is the quickest way to England, the Channel Tunnel notwithstanding.

left: **Les Pirouettes du Vieux Moulin,** DISNEYLAND RESORT PARIS

A Disneyland Resort Paris exclusive, this Fantasyland Ferris wheel is attached to a Dutch-inspired windmill. Guests enjoy a bird's-eye view of Alice's Curious Labyrinth and the roofs of Fantasyland while riding in giant water buckets.

left: **Soarin',** WALT DISNEY WORLD RESORT

The newest addition to The Land pavilion at *Epcot*®, scheduled to take off in 2005, lifts guests high into a massive projection screen dome for an exhilarating flight above the Golden State. Combining wraparound cinematography and state-of-the-art motion technology, Soarin' completely surrounds passengers with the sights, sounds, and scents of California—all as they float forty feet above the ground.

below: **Soarin' Over California,** DISNEY'S CALIFORNIA ADVENTURE

Watch your toes! You're about to graze the Golden Gate Bridge. Passengers on this Disney's California Adventure simulated hang glider swoop and soar in front of a curving, eighty-foot-wide movie screen. The illusion of flight is complete as they fly over Golden State landmarks, such as Yosemite, Tahoe, Palm Springs, even Disneyland. Along the way, gliders feel the wind in their hair, get spritzed with sea spray, and are tantalized by the fragrance of ripe oranges.

above: **Flik's Flyers,** Disney's California Adventure

Flik, the forever-clever ant from *A Bug's Life*, has fashioned floating balloons from twigs and leaves for this kid-friendly attraction at Disney's California Adventure.

left: **TriceraTop Spin,** Walt Disney World Resort

At Chester & Hester's Dino-Rama!, the roadside attraction in DinoLand U.S.A., a flying dino-go-round spins young riders back to the Cretaceous Era.

The Barnstormer at Goofy's Wiseacre Farm,
WALT DISNEY WORLD RESORT

The first kid-sized roller coaster at Walt Disney World (built in 1996) is as goofy as its namesake. In an out-of-control crop duster, passengers whip over rows of tomatoes and cotton, then crash through the side of a farm building. Barnstormer, indeed.

above & left: **Maliboomer,** Disney's California Adventure
top right: **Jumpin' Jellyfish,** Disney's California Adventure

Maliboomer looks like an oversized version of those old swing-the-sledgehammer, ring-the-bell midway games—way oversized! At 180-feet-tall it towers over the park. After shooting to the top in less than three seconds, guests free fall down again in an eye blink. If they manage to keep their eyes open, the view from the top is fantastic. Jumpin' Jellyfish, a kid-friendly version of Maliboomer, rockets riders 60 feet in the air, then slowly bounces them back to earth under jellyfish umbrellas.

WILD AT HEART

Disney has always had a soft spot for nature and the furry creatures that fill it. Think of *The Lion King, Bambi,* and *The Jungle Book.* From animated classics to short cartoons to films such as the True-Life Adventures series of the 1950s, humanity's four-legged friends have a way of getting top billing in studio productions. And why not? After all, the whole enterprise started with a mouse, as Walt once famously said. In the years since Mickey made his silver screen debut in "Steamboat Willie" in 1928, the Disney menagerie has grown by leaps, bounds, hops, and jumps, fleshing out films and filling the richly planted parks. To visit Walt Disney World today is to take a walk on the wild side: you never know what you might encounter around the next bend in the path.

Tree of Life, WALT DISNEY WORLD RESORT

Rising 145 feet above Discovery Island, hub of Disney's Animal Kingdom, the iconic tree celebrates nature's awe-inspiring diversity. More than 300 elaborate animal carvings cover its massive trunk from branch tips to roots, a magical expression of every living thing's place in the circle of life. The entwined images include lions, whales, bats, and a very well-known chimpanzee.

Discovery Island Trails, WALT DISNEY WORLD RESORT

A lush habitat of pools and meadows spreads outward from the Tree of Life, home to an amazing mix of wildlife. On Discovery Island Trails, red kangaroos hop through the underbrush; Galápagos tortoises laze in the sun, and macaws survey their kingdom from perches in the trees. A favorite guest pastime is to identify animals carved on the Tree of Life, then seek out their real-life counterparts on the surrounding trails.

Pangani Forest Exploration Trail, WALT DISNEY WORLD RESORT
In Swahili, Pangani means "place of enchantment." And so
it is; this jungle trail begins in the village of Harambe in the
Africa section of Disney's Animal Kingdom. On a self-guided
tour, hikers observe exotic animals in nature. Among the highlights: a pack of meerkats in the Timon exhibit (but don't
expect them to sing), giraffes and antelopes grazing on the
savanna, and a family of magnificent lowland gorillas.

Amid stone ruins and forgotten gardens, trekkers in this corner of Asia at Disney's Animal Kingdom encounter piglike tapirs, cave-dwelling giant fruit bats, and Komodo dragons—at up to twelve feet long, they are the earth's largest lizards. But the true stars are the Asian tigers, regal as the maharajah whose abandoned estate they now rule.

opposite: **Swiss Family Treehouse,** WALT DISNEY WORLD RESORT

An arboreal curiosity, the *Disneyodendron eximus* (roughly, "out-of-the-ordinary Disney tree") towers over Adventureland, providing sanctuary to the castaway clan of the 1960 Disney live-action film *Swiss Family Robinson*. Some 800,000 plastic leaves sprout from the 1,400 branches of the tree, which is made of 200 tons of steel and concrete. High in the canopy, the Robinsons have rigged a penthouse apartment of a tree fort, complete with running water courtesy of a clever waterwheel-and-bucket delivery system.

above & top: **Festival of the Lion King,** WALT DISNEY WORLD RESORT

Can you feel the love tonight? It's impossible not to at this acrobatic Lion King dance and song spectacular. Presented in the round at a covered theater in Camp Minnie-Mickey at Disney's Animal Kingdom, the thirty-minute Broadway-style pageant celebrates the circle of life.

Redwood Creek Challenge Trail, DISNEY'S CALIFORNIA ADVENTURE

From the lookout towers of Redwood Creek Challenge Trail at Disney's California Adventure, children glide like flying squirrels on 60-foot zip lines. Inspired by the West's great national parks, the outdoor play area also features springy suspension bridges, bouncy cargo nets, a cave to hide in, and a hollowed-out redwood tree to explore.

above & right: **The Living Seas,** WALT DISNEY WORLD RESORT

Where is the world's largest saltwater aquarium? If you said *Epcot*®, you're right. Holding nearly six million gallons, the tank teems with marine life at The Living Seas. Among the 3,000 or so residents: sharks, barracudas, rays, angelfish, and dolphins.

below: **The Land,** WALT DISNEY WORLD RESORT

Epcot®'s largest pavilion covers six acres and produces more than 30 tons of fruit and vegetables every year. In addition to being the breadbasket of *Epcot*® (much of the produce is served at the park's restaurants), The Land includes interactive attractions such as Living with the Land, an ecotour by boat of the pavilion's rain forests, prairies, and farm environments.

A
WONDERFUL
WORLD

It may be a small world in terms of shared hopes and dreams, but practically speaking, it's a pretty big place—the world of Disney, that is. Wild and wonderful, it covers thousands of acres of land and stretches out even further in time, spanning the yesterdays of Main Street, U.S.A., and the tomorrows of *Epcot*®, whose name is an acronym of "Experimental Prototype Community of Tomorrow." It contains many lands, a kingdom that's pure magic, and even a world within a world, where eleven countries are replicated in scale. Mostly, though, Disney is a world of wonder, a one-of-a-kind place whose only borders are the limits of imagination.

"it's a small world," WALT DISNEY WORLD RESORT

The year was 1964. Walt Disney had just created a global village of singing dolls for the New York World's Fair. The attraction had the charm of an enchanted toy store, but Walt needed a good song to make it really special. Wisely, he turned to the legendary songwriting brothers Richard and Robert Sherman, whose music for *Mary Poppins* would soon win them a pair of Oscars. The rest, as they say, is history. "It's A Small World (After All)" became an all-time favorite Disney tune, and the heart and soul of an attraction that's as beguiling today as when it made its Walt Disney World debut in 1971.

overleaf & clockwise: **"it's a small world,"** DISNEYLAND, DISNEYLAND RESORT PARIS, TOKYO DISNEYLAND
Every quarter-hour, a parade of characters marches around the clock tower that dominates the impressive facade of the Disneyland "it's a small world." Inside, 297 children and 256 toys represent 100 parts of the world. The Tokyo Disneyland version, dating to 1983, repeats Disneyland's long exterior. At Disneyland Resort Paris, the marquee is similar to those in Tokyo and Anaheim, but the show ends with The World Chorus, featuring a miniature city of international buildings wherein children sing the theme song one last time.

141

World Showcase, WALT DISNEY WORLD RESORT

At World Showcase, the world truly is at your fingertips. Eleven countries are
represented in concentrated form, with the character of each revealed through
architecture, cuisine, art, and people. Traveling through it is like poring over
a photo album of a special vacation. You get the monuments, buildings, and shops
in living color—the landmarks that capture a place's essence.

right: **Canada,** WALT DISNEY WORLD RESORT

From the seagoing Maritime Provinces in the east, across the Rocky Mountains, to the lush gardens of famously temperate Victoria, British Columbia, in the west, Canada celebrates the geographic diversity of North America's largest country. Ethnic diversity, too: English, French, and Celtic are strong influences here, the latter in the form of Off Kilter, a hard-driving, tartan skirt–wearing band that somehow makes bagpipes rock.

below: **United Kingdom,** WALT DISNEY WORLD RESORT

Ah, to be in England. Cobbled city streets, half-timbered Tudor buildings, and thatch-roofed country cottages—all in the space of a few hundred feet. Strolling from London to the countryside, tourists pass High Street shops stocked with bone china, hand-knit sweaters, exotic teas, and other British imports. Follow the accents to Rose & Crown Pub, a favorite haunt of English expatriates and anyone else who savors a perfect pint.

Cinema connoisseurs say the wide-screen film *Impressions de France* ranks as one of *Epcot*®'s best experiences. The movie takes viewers on an armchair tour of the country, from romantic Paris to sun-drenched Provence and beyond. Connoisseurs of a different sort flock to Les Vins du France, a world-class wine shop not far from this France's small-scale Eiffel Tower.

The replica of Koutoubia Minaret, a Marrakesh landmark, stands as one of World Showcase's architectural wonders. To create its elaborate mosaics, 23 Moroccan artisans applied nine tons of hand-cut tiles to wet plaster. In the shadow of the prayer tower, alleys and courtyards transport guests to North Africa.

bottom left: **Japan,** WALT DISNEY WORLD RESORT

The five stories of the Goju-no-to pagoda symbolize earth, water, fire, wind, and sky. The elements are in harmony throughout this peaceful land, on winding paths amid traditional gardens and in the balanced architecture of Mitsukoshi Department Store, modeled after the Imperial Palace in Kyoto.

top right & bottom right: **Italy,** WALT DISNEY WORLD RESORT

From atop the Campanile in Italy, an angel gazes down on crowds in a broad plaza. Like the original in Venice's Piazza San Marco, this 100-foot-high statue is leafed in real gold. A similar attention to detail prevails throughout the pavilion, right down to the traditional gondolas tied up to red-striped poles in the World Showcase Lagoon.

Germany, WALT DISNEY WORLD RESORT

With its arches, turrets, and balconies, Germany seems to be a fairy tale come to life. In fact, the architecture is a realistic blend of cities and towns throughout Germany. Equally accurate is the bustling outdoor beer garden, modeled after the site of Munich's legendary Oktoberfest.

China, WALT DISNEY WORLD RESORT

"May good fortune follow you on your path through life." So translate characters on a banner at the Gate of the Golden Sun, entrance to China. Fortune definitely smiles on this pavilion, where the Circle-Vision 360 film *Reflections of China* offers a feast for the eyes, while Nine Dragons Restaurant serves up a gastronomic one. Another treat is the preview center for Hong Kong Disneyland, where guests can check out plans for the first Disney theme park in the pavilion's namesake country.

Norway, WALT DISNEY WORLD RESORT

In Maelstrom, Norway pavilion's "E" ticket attraction, visitors set off in a dragon-headed Viking longboat for what is supposed to be a gentle cruise. As the boat passes through a mystical Norwegian forest, however, trolls send it plunging backward for a wild ride through a whirlpool and into the past.

Mexico, WALT DISNEY WORLD RESORT

Within a Mayan pyramid, travelers find El Río del Tiempo: The River of Time. The twilight-lit boat trip uses film, intricate stage sets, and Audio-Animatronics to showcase the culture of Mexico. Guests float past a pre-Columbian temple, a folk dance, and a cheerily macabre Day of the Dead celebration, complete with a skeleton band. Outside the attraction, actual living mariachis perform in the plaza.

opposite: **IllumiNations: Reflections of Earth,** WALT DISNEY WORLD RESORT
Lasers etch the night sky, fireworks explode in color, and fountains erupt above
the shimmering surface of World Showcase Lagoon. Together, the elemental
components of fire and water tell a story as epic as life itself: nothing less
than the history of the planet. Every explosion of fireworks is timed to the
beat of an original symphonic score that incorporates rhythms from around
the world.

above: **World Bazaar,** TOKYO DISNEYLAND
Where Walt Disney World fans might expect to find Main Street, U.S.A.,
Tokyo Disneyland features the World Bazaar, an elegant glass-canopied
shopping district. Aside from featuring a Victorian conservatory-style structure,
which frames Cinderella Castle, the area looks very much like a picture-perfect
nineteenth-century American town.

TO INFINITY AND BEYOND!

From ancient sailors who gazed at the stars and saw mythological creatures, to modern rocket scientists who design and launch deep-space rovers, humans have always found fascination in the distant heavens. That tradition of looking upward for inspiration is alive and well at Walt Disney World and has been ever since the Magic Kingdom opened with Tomorrowland as one of its original realms. In the Disney galaxy, potently realistic experiences (Mission: SPACE) combine with purely fanciful ones (Buzz Lightyear's Space Ranger Spin) to create an alternate reality. Call it the universe of fun, a place where earthbound adventurers are encouraged to shoot for the stars.

Space Mountain, WALT DISNEY WORLD RESORT

The original roller coaster on rocket fuel, Space Mountain at Magic Kingdom Park altered the rules for thrill rides when it opened in 1975. For one thing, it's housed inside a 180-foot-tall lunar landscape of a building. For another, it takes place in inky darkness. Unable to see what's coming, riders can only strap in, cross their fingers, and scream for all they're worth as they blast into the great unknown.

Space Mountain, DISNEYLAND

On the occasion of Disneyland's 50th Anniversary in 2005, a new generation of special effects was added to Space Mountain, including a launch sequence that gives guests a hair-raising encounter with a meteorite. Additionally, the perennial favorite got new rocket vehicles, a fresh sound track blasted over an upgraded sound system, and a longer re-entry tunnel packed with dazzling lights in addition to a gleaming new exterior. Final verdict: Space Mountain blasts into the twenty-first century.

opposite top left: **Space Mountain,** Tokyo Disneyland
opposite top right & bottom: **Space Mountain,** Disneyland Resort Paris

Space Mountain roared into Tokyo Disneyland in 1983 and landed at Disneyland Resort Paris in 1995, on the twentieth anniversary of the original. In France, it features a 72-foot-long cannon that shoots riders to the summit in less than two seconds.

above: **Mission: SPACE,** Walt Disney World Resort

Would-be space cowboys are strapped side by side into the tight cockpit of an X-2 flight pod for a rocket ride to Mars. As they race to complete assigned crew tasks, astronauts experience mega Gs at liftoff and sheer terror during a meteor bombardment. Unearthly thrills? Mission accomplished.

chapter opener: **Astro Orbiter,** WALT DISNEY WORLD; opposite: **Astro Orbitor** DISNEYLAND; left: **Orbitron—*Machines Volantes,*** DISNEYLAND RESORT PARIS

THE FUTURE THAT NEVER WAS IS FINALLY HERE. So says the sign at the entrance to Tomorrowland. Case in point: the Astro Orbiter, seemingly straight off the pages of a sci-fi fantasy. With a slight spelling change, the stylized rocket ride also anchors Tomorrowland at Disneyland, providing sky-high park views as riders shoot past planets. Like its American cousins, the version at Disneyland Resort Paris Discoveryland, known as Orbitron—*Machines Volantes* (Flying Machines), is inspired in part by the futuristic sketchbooks of Leonardo da Vinci.

below: **StarJets,** TOKYO DISNEYLAND

At Tokyo Disneyland, the Orbiter remains StarJets, as the spinning rocket ships at Walt Disney World were originally called. They also retain the sleek, white, spaceship styling.

Star Tours, Walt Disney World Resort

The Moon of Endor: basically a puddle jump away, right? Sure, if everything goes according to schedule. Which it naturally doesn't during this *Star Wars–* inspired fantasy. Featuring an FX-crammed film seamlessly synched to an advanced, military-style flight simulator, Star Tours blasts groups of forty interstellar commuters into deepest space. With rookie pilot REX at the controls, the Star Speeder spaceship encounters enemy fighters and mammoth ice crystals, among other hair-raising obstacles. Where's Luke Skywalker when you need him?

opposite: Spaceship Earth, Walt Disney World Resort

Many know it simply as "the Ball"—the gleaming geosphere that rises above *Epcot®* like a silvery planet. Visible from throughout Walt Disney World, Spaceship Earth seems to grow as you draw near, until standing beneath it, you finally appreciate its true immensity—180 feet tall, 515 feet around, and more than 16 million pounds.

opposite inset: Spaceship Earth (interior), Walt Disney World Resort

The dimpled skin of Spaceship Earth wraps around two million cubic feet of space, ample room to stage a magical history tour. Smithsonian scholars and science-fiction writer Ray Bradbury were among the many consultants who helped Disney Imagineers put together this attraction, in which time travelers proceed from the dawn of civilization to the twenty-first century as they spiral up the inside of the geosphere. Along the way, detailed scenes trace the evolution of communication technology from cave paintings to television and beyond.

Golden Zephyr, DISNEY'S CALIFORNIA ADVENTURE

Suspended by cables from an 85-foot-high tower, Golden Zephyr's stainless steel rockets swing above Disney's California Adventure like moonbeams. Sleek and elegant, they're less about far-off future galaxies and more about a not-so-distant past of carnival fun.

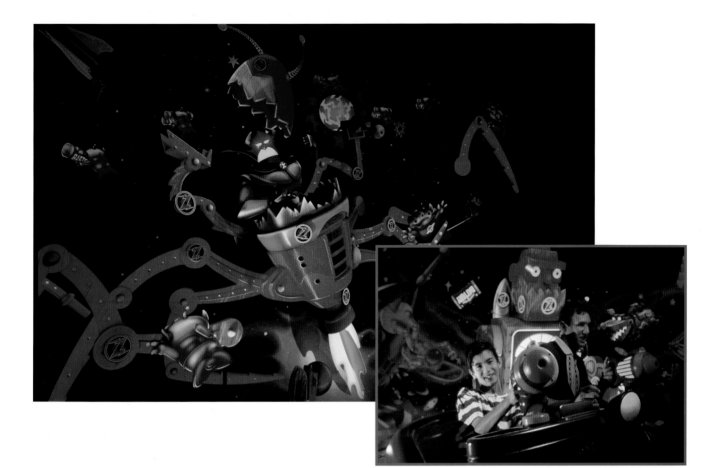

above: **Buzz Lightyear's Space Ranger Spin,** WALT DISNEY WORLD RESORT

Evil Zurg is on the rampage. To stop the *Toy Story* archfiend, Junior Space Rangers blast away at his minions from star cruisers loaded with laser cannons. Hitting targets triggers special effects in this immersive adventure—equal parts ride, video game, and animated movie.

below: **Stitch's Great Escape!,** WALT DISNEY WORLD RESORT

Before turning over a new leaf as a lovable lapdog, the star of the newest and most sophisticated Audio-Animatronics adventure at Tomorrowland was known as "Experiment 626": mayhem in a pint-sized package. The family-friendly attraction takes place prior to the events of the movie, when Stitch is first revealed in all his mischievous glory.

SHOW

At Disney, as nowhere else, the show truly must go on. Make that
shows. Dozens and dozens are mounted every day throughout the
parks, on stages large and small, indoors and out, with human
actors, Audio-Animatronics, animation, and performing animals
all cast in leading roles. Using every trick of the storyteller's art
(and inventing new ones as needed), Disney dream weavers lift
fantasies off the movie screen and bring them to life in three
dimensions. Like all great theater, Disney's shows tug at heart-
strings, tickle funny bones, and present unforgettable spectacles.
They amuse, delight, and amaze, and they do so within enchanted
environments, where every Park is a stage set in itself and magic
is always in the air.

Mickey's PhilharMagic, WALT DISNEY WORLD RESORT

A collaboration between Walt Disney Imagineering and Feature Animation, the newest 3-D film at Walt Disney World takes guests on a magical tour of Disney animated features, using music, puppetry, and dazzling special effects to project the action into the audience. In one scene, dancing brooms splash water at Donald Duck, but it's the viewers who wind up wet. In another, a large apple pie sweeps through the theater, fresh-baked aroma and all.

top: ***Honey, I Shrunk the Audience,*** Walt Disney World Resort

Do my eyes deceive me? Well, yes. Those mice and other creatures flying off the screen do not really exist. Not in three dimensions, they don't. Nor are audience members actually reduced to the size of raisins in this 3-D theatrical based on the hit movies. It just feels that way. Boy, does it feel that way.

above left: ***It's Tough To Be A Bug!,*** Walt Disney World
above right: ***It's Tough to be a Bug!,*** Disney's California Adventure

Squeamish viewers have been known to bug out at this *Bug's Life*–inspired extravaganza in Disney's Animal Kingdom Tree of Life Theater. Such is the power of 3-D film, especially when it's enhanced by in-theater special effects. If you think the Chilean tarantula is something, just wait for the stinkbug. It'll really take your breath away. At Disney's California Adventure, *It's Tough to be a Bug!* plays in a custom-built theater in a bug's land.

Muppet*Vision 3D, WALT DISNEY WORLD RESORT

Eye-popping 3-D effects are just the beginning. Also deserving star billing are the Muppets; physical special effects, including huge soap bubbles, squirting lapel flowers, and rushing wind; and, of course, the Disney-MGM theater itself. A perfect replica of the original *Muppet Show* set, the jewel box even features hecklers Statler and Waldorf—tart as ever up in their balcony.

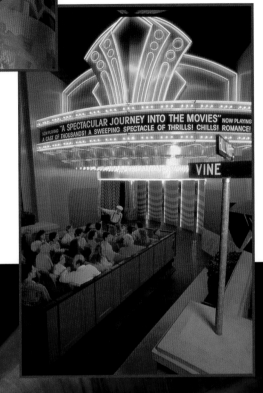

The Great Movie Ride, WALT DISNEY WORLD RESORT

A must for any movie lover. A tram spirits guests into Audio-Animatronics re-creations of some of the most memorable scenes in film history. You can almost feel the raindrops during the dance through puddles in *Singin' in the Rain*. Bullets fly in a Gangster Alley shoot-up in *Public Enemy*. The monster slithers overhead in *Alien*. And when Rick and Ilsa say farewell in *Casablanca*, guests are right on the runway with them. Many of the props are Hollywood originals, including a pair of Dorothy's ruby slippers from *The Wizard of Oz*.

The Enchanted Tiki Room—Under New Management, WALT DISNEY WORLD RESORT
The original Enchanted Tiki Room made history as Disneyland's first Audio-Animatronics attraction in 1963 with more than 200 warbling parrots, plants, and totems. Longtime headliners Michael, Fritz, Pierre, and José are still in this updated incarnation, where Iago, from *Aladdin,* and *The Lion King's* Zazu take over and cause enough trouble to make the goddess Uh-Oa cause a little explosive payback.

above: **Country Bear Jamboree,** WALT DISNEY WORLD RESORT

These grizzled veterans of the country music scene may well be the world's longest-running jam band. They've been playing to sold-out houses in Grizzly Hall, the Grand Ole Opry of the back country, since 1971. Under the direction of Henry, the coonskin cap–wearing emcee, furry favorites Big Al and Teddi Barra, among a cave-full of others, swap jokes and share songs as they mug through a crowd-pleasing set.

left: **Country Bear Theater,** TOKYO DISNEYLAND

At Tokyo Disneyland, Bunny, Bubbles, Beulah, and the rest of the gang stage their review in Westernland's Country Bear Theater. Like their American cousins, the bears perform two seasonal shows—the Jingle Bell Jamboree and the Vacation Jamboree—as well as their standard set.

above: **Hyperion Theater,** DISNEY'S CALIFORNIA ADVENTURE

With 2,000 plush seats, sweeping double balconies, and a rich gold-and-red color scheme, the majestic Hyperion Theater at Disney's California Adventure has the look and feel of an Art Deco historic landmark. Don't be fooled by all the gilt. Beneath the gorgeous surface, the theater has state-of-the-art mechanical systems that are the envy of Broadway.

chapter opener & opposite: **SpectroMagic,** WALT DISNEY WORLD RESORT

Laid end to end, SpectroMagic's 100 miles of fiber-optic cables and threads would stretch from Orlando to Tampa—and a third of the way back again. The glorious parade's 600,000 miniature bulbs could light a highway. Fortunately, they're used for nothing so mundane. Twinkling in perfect harmony with a rousing score, the points of light trace hypnotic patterns around floats bearing Disney characters down Main Street, U.S.A., in this most beloved of nighttime spectacles.

Fantasmic!, WALT DISNEY WORLD RESORT

The M-I-C in the title refers to Mickey, of course, whose dreams come to life in this stunning water-and-light show at Disney-MGM Studios. In the guise of the *Fantasia* sorcerer, Mickey conjures up a world of dancing fountains, shooting stars, and larger-than-life Disney characters, including a host of villains who attempt to hijack his dreams. When he musters the full force of his imagination, it's lights out for the bad guys.

Wishes Nighttime Spectacular, WALT DISNEY WORLD RESORT

"You know, any wish is possible—it just takes a little courage to set it free," says Jiminy Cricket, narrator of Magic Kingdom Park's newest fireworks show. He could be talking about the display itself. With more than 650 individual fireworks, appearances around the castle by eleven Disney characters, and a dozen songs from six different animated films all choreographed to within 1/30th of a second of the explosions, Wishes is Disney's boldest pyrotechnics show ever. Aim for the stars, the nighttime spectacle urges. Wishes do come true. At this magical place, they come true every day.

INDEX: ATTRACTIONS BY PARK

176